RISING

IN

AMERICA

BY

ALEX REZENDE

Ordering Information: Quantity sales. Special discounts are available on quantity purchases by corporations, associations, and others. Orders by U.S. trade bookstores and wholesalers.

DREAMSTARTERS

www.DreamStartersPublishing.com

Table of Contents

Introduction

I'm an immigrant. I moved to the United States at the age of 18 and didn't know where to start or what to do. Over the years, I have felt the desire to tell my story for those that follow behind me on their own journey. There were so many questions. What will happen to me? Where will I end up? How can I adapt into society and live a full and productive life while still giving back to this country? There is not one path, but many.

My story is a classic American Dream success story -- a young immigrant comes to this country with just two cardboard boxes as belongings without being able to speak the language and, through hard work and determination, becomes successful in his profession. I want to share my story as a way to give back and to give hope and inspiration to other immigrants just beginning. It can be done! But there are so many necessary steps to take to get there. I will talk about how I did it, but this book is not just about hard work, it is also about dreams.

Real estate is my chosen profession, it is like any profession, there is no magic formula or secret sauce for financial success; it is mostly grit and perseverance, given the opportunity, and a lot of support from friends, managers, and family thrown in. Just like you, I am not always excited to get up each day and think about goals, but keeping your eyes looking forward is one of the critical components of success. Imagine yourself traveling across the world on a boat or plane without a map or a GPS. You need a "road map a guide."

I believe the most important part of the journey is what you learn along the way. Yes, I love having the money to buy what I want and go where I please, but I learned that there are much more important things in life. These are the lessons I want to share with you, not the particulars of my profession. There are many ways to become rich, but achieving success is not about wealth. This may sound cliché, I know, I heard it many times before and thought to myself "Yeah right," but it is true. I became more successful in life and in business when I stopped worrying about things and just started enjoying them.

I think an analogy for this is my journey in Tae Kwon Do. When I was eight years old, I started studying this ancient martial art. Unfortunately, my mom ran out of money, and things go really tight, so I had to stop. This broke my heart, really, because it became a huge part of me, almost to the point of being how I identified myself at that young age. But, there was nothing I could do about it. I had to just move on in my life. But, I never gave up on my dream and goal of pursuing Tae Kwon Do.

After many years, I went back, as an adult, and started my pursuit of becoming a master at Tae Kwon Do. Before that, I explored other martial arts, but they never meant as

5

much as Tae Kwon Do did to me. I couldn't when I was a child because we had run out of money, mom was divorced with three young kids, and like many moms in this position, things were hard. When I was finally able to get back into it, it was like a dream. I also wanted to get back into working out, and staying fit and healthy, so it was a natural fit that would help me reach several goals.

The local gym that I went to didn't have an adult program, only one for kids. Now, even though I felt like a big kid at that point, reliving my childhood pursuit, we knew that we had to come up with something different. So, we created a program where I would meet with Master Song, one-on-one. Later, a few others joined the program. I started back as a white belt since I had been out of practice for so long, but after about a year and a half of lots of work and many hours, I finally received my black belt.

The day that I received that belt, and put it on for the first time, I saw my dream from childhood come true. I had set a goal and reached it. Not in the timeframe that I envisioned, nor in the way that I thought I would, but I had reached that goal. I stopped worrying about how much time it was taking, and how much money it was costing. I enjoyed the pursuit of that goal, of that dream. And, now, looking back, I see that in a way I was in pursuit of a continuation of achieving the American dream.

ALEX REZENDE

Through the martial arts, I learned discipline, meditation techniques, and how to be at peace with the present. But, the biggest lesson I learned was how to stick with something. I learned that I could persevere, even though circumstances in my past hadn't allowed me to pursue this dream. If I had given up on that one dream, that one goal of achieving a black belt in Tae Kwon Do, in many ways I would have been giving up on myself, and what I could achieve in my new country. Studying martial arts, in a very real way, gave me the confidence I needed to put my best foot forward every day in my new country and community.

My wish and hope for you is that you become part of this great country and participate fully in its rich culture. To do that, you will need to change who you are and become someone different -- an American. This does not mean you lose all that you had, rather it's like gaining a new family. To be accepted here, it's important to adapt, learn the language and become part of the community. It's that simple but certainly not easy.

Here is how I did it. I know that it is possible to "Rise in America" and I hope my words can provide inspiration for those who are fearless and ready to take off.

This is my story.

"If you want to go somewhere, it is best to find someone who has already been there."

Robert Kiyosaki

Chapter One

FEAR

I was a young man in Brazil, a decent student approaching my final year of high school, when my parents approached me with the idea of moving to the United States. Dad lived in the States with my step-mom and I was living a typical teenage life in Brazil at home with my mom. Both my parents felt that the opportunities for success and growth were much greater for me if I moved and started fresh in the U.S. before beginning a career.

I remember around this time I still had a bit of a fantasy of becoming a famous soccer player, what young Brazilian boy doesn't? But I had a revelation and changed my dream. I lived in Sao Paulo, one of the largest cities in the world. I would go to Avenida Paulista, the business district, and watch the businessmen in their fine suits bustle along the busy streets. I imagined a famous soccer player walking on the same road and being mobbed by fans, his fame preceding him. Yet, the CEO of a company, can make millions and still be anonymous and live life without all the scrutiny. I decided right then I would rather be a CEO than a famous soccer player!

The United States is considered the land of opportunity, where entrepreneurship and the freedom to become who and what you dream of are within reach. I was fortunate to be from Brazil, where we have freedom to come and go and do as we please. But, if you reach a certain level of success in Brazil, there will be someone there who wants to collect some "protection money" from you. This is a common problem in many countries and much worse in many other South American countries. It can put fear in your heart and keep you down and afraid to really put yourself out there.

It reminds me of a story I heard about elephants in India. They tie them to trees when they are babies and not strong enough to just tear the tree down and be free. After many years of captivity, the elephants are full grown and powerful, but remained tied to the tree because they do not believe they can tear it down. This can happen to immigrants coming to this country as well. They have lived so long in fear, they don't try to fly free once they get here.

I was hesitant at first. I had a nice circle of friends, and a life that I was happy with. But I felt an opportunity that kept calling me and I knew that this was the time. After much

10

discussion with my parents and a lot of self-reflection, I decided to take the plunge into the unknown! **I moved to AMERICA.**

The first thing I had to learn was how to live here and blend in. Fear lived with me constantly in those early days. I didn't know the language and that made basic, everyday things almost impossible. Just getting across what you wanted to eat was a challenge. I always feared being ridiculed but mostly I felt left behind. It's difficult to make friends when you cannot understand the conversations around you -- it's lonely. There were times people tried to talk with me but at the end of the day, if you can't communicate, people will move on. I saw how others had come here with the same dream only to get stuck in a low-paying job with no way out. I didn't want that to be me; I wanted to make a difference and be a success. I knew that school and learning the language were essential to obtaining a better life.

When I started school, I was placed back in sophomore year even though I should have been a senior. I felt embarrassed to be 18 and just a sophomore and yet, I had to spend 6-8 hours at home studying by myself after classes, learning the vocabulary and trying to get my head around what was going on in my classes. Language is a powerful tool that can teach you new things, allows you to communicate with others and eventually, even allows you to influence people to make big changes in their lives. Step by step, I moved forward.

There are some many things against you when you first get here and they seem to get harder and increase day by day. Things you really don't even think about until you are confronted by them. Of course, I expected people to look at me and have an impression of me that was based on being different, but I didn't realize how isolating it would be. I didn't understand the culture, the jokes, the signs, you name it. It was terrifying to try to order something to eat and not understand a simple question about it. I didn't even understand the money and how much things cost. The weather was even a new and stressful thing for me to get acquainted with, not to mention the food!

I made a decision in that first year, I knew that I had to change into a new person if I was going to succeed in this country. I had to let go of my old self and adapt to my life. I couldn't continue watching my Brazilian shows and listening to Brazilian music and expect anyone to relate to me. I needed to begin to identify with my new country and adopt its language and its culture. Everything around me had changed and I needed to adapt or live in isolation! I had to get a grip. Slowly, I opened up and allowed the changes. When kids would talk about a new tv show or a sports team, I would watch the TV show or the game so I could be part of that conversation. It was hard to put myself out there like that but I forced myself to do it. I still followed my favorite Brazilian soccer team, but I also followed my American Football team.

I started to love and appreciate my new country and the people around me. *America is an amazing place to live*, but I came to see that, if you are not in a good place with yourself, it doesn't matter where you live, you will never be happy or successful. Paradise is not a place, it's a state of mind; paradise occurs when you are happy. When you go on vacation you feel like you are in paradise, but it's not the location, it's how you look at it. Yes, the view helps, but it is truly about being happy and in a good place with yourself.

If your desire is to have a dream of success and accomplishment in your new country, start by looking inside yourself. America is not perfect, there are always good and bad in all things and places. The important thing is to learn how to become part of the system and make the most of it. That can only be done by loving your new home and giving back to the community however you can.

Think about how you reflect yourself to others, they want to understand who you are and why you are here, but they really don't. It's your job to make the people and the community richer for having you there. Not in terms of money, and not by thinking you know a better way personally as well as professionally. Instead, you make the community richer in terms of giving back to others, in actions, in ideas, and by respecting the culture.

13

Yes, some people will be suspicious of you and your motives, but who cares? If you carry on about your old country and how great everything was there, they may think, "If it was so great there, why don't you just go back?" Can you blame them? You are the one that needs to adapt, not everyone around you.

It's fine to talk to people about your country, but don't just brag about how beautiful everything was there. There is no right or wrong way to do things, it's important to understand that there are many ways to do things, not just your way. I have traveled much of the Southern U.S. and each state believes they have the best barbeque ribs. Well, they are actually all good, just different! Remember to respect the traditions in your community and you will gain respect.

There are times when it can get frustrating and discouraging and you'll want to give up and go back to what you know. Save some of your prior life to retreat to at times; it helps with the adjustment. I found comfort following my Brazilian soccer teams when I needed a break from the stress. It is ok, only natural. The important thing is to be open to more than what you are used to.

I never stopped seeing the potential of what I could become here. Keeping my eye on the future and its potential, helped me get through some of the tough times. There were many of those moments, it happens to all of us, It definitely helped me with the constant fear that surrounded me during those early years.

There was no single moment when everything transformed, but many small moments that gave me encouragement. High school was tough, but finishing was a huge accomplishment and I worked hard learning the language during that time.

I had been placed in an "English as a Second Language" classroom where most of the students spoke Spanish. But being from Brazil, my native language is Portuguese. I found myself attempting to communicate in Spanish since the languages are so similar -- but I didn't want to learn Spanish, I wanted to **learn English**. I decided to request placement in the main English-speaking classes where I felt I could learn the language faster. This change forced me to focus on English every minute of every day and then most of the evening too! For me, it worked. By the time I graduated from high school, I was able to communicate enough to make my thoughts understood.

Building up confidence is the polar opposite of fear, and I think that's where so much of my early life in the United States came from. Making it as an immigrant in the United States, for me, was letting go of my fears, and having confidence in myself and in those around me. As a new immigrant, not knowing the language, my confidence was the lowest it has ever been. But, I had to build that back up, step by step. Even into adulthood.

It's easy to assume that adults around us are walking around with all the confidence that they need, but I find that often the opposite is true. Most adults have some insecurities and things in their lives that they are not confident about. This is natural, and it shouldn't be something that brings you down further. You're not alone, and we've all been there, to some extent or another.

Finding a way to build your confidence and overcome fear is critical to being a successful immigrant in this country, or any country, for that matter. It's also critical to becoming a successful person. Pursuing your dreams and goals, no holds barred, and trusting in yourself to get things done, in their own time.

"The key to success is to focus our conscious mind on things we desire not things we fear."

Brian Tracy

START RISING

What do you fear?

_____

_____

_____

_____

How have your fears held you back?

_____

_____

_____

_____

How can you shed your fears so that you can live your true potential?

_____

_____

_____

_____

Chapter Two

How to Adjust to and Live in the U.S.

Once I graduated and began getting out and meeting people and doing things, I started to feel more a part of society and to really "live" here. You have to live it! America is a breathing and living soul full of wonderful things to enjoy and benefit from. That is exactly why you moved here; not to keep holding on to your past or your country and its beliefs and culture.

You need to merge and adapt. You don't have to forget or abandon what and who you are but instead, grow into someone even better than before. Someone who is world-traveled and experienced and can bring those experiences to the table.

19

Become involved in all the wonderful things the U.S. has to offer; from cultural, sporting, and social events, to business and religious organizations and more. Whatever your interests are, become part of that society and all the wonderful things it has to offer. Find your common ground, where people speak your language and share your culture, but don't isolate yourself there. Get out of your comfort zone and force yourself to experience new things and to meet new people. New friends I made have enlightened my life and made it much easier for me to feel at home.

If you find yourself reading about cars, then go out to events about cars. You have to find your own way and develop your passions. I had many passions and followed them here in the states. I enjoy Tae Kwon Do, skydiving, scuba-diving, zip-lining and race-car driving. Of course, I could not afford those things at first, but I did what I could to be part of a group of people with my interests. The best thing you can do is to get yourself out in your community enjoying whatever it is you love. They call it immersion for a reason, **jump in**!

What I often see now are people just learning enough to get by, "Where's the bathroom?, How much does this cost?" Once they learn the basics needed to get around, they stop learning and stay in their little bubble with people who speak their language. They think they can come here and take without giving back; however, they must learn the culture and then re-invent themselves.

This is bad for them and bad for society. It's necessary to do the work and learn the language, beyond the basics. To do that, you can't just read it or study. You need to get out there and listen to the way people communicate and speak up! You will make a lot of mistakes but that is the only way to learn. I know so many people that can read English but no-one can understand a word they are saying when they open their mouths because they have not made the effort to practice, practice, practice. Don't get complacent -- once you learn to navigate the basics, never stop learning and studying the language. You need to go all in with whatever you are doing, whether it's learning the language, developing relationships or working at a new job.

When I was in high school, I would come home and write down all the new words that I learned that day in my vocabulary book. My goal, beyond that, was to learn 10-20 new words a week, really learn them by using them in conversation and writing, not just memorizing them. I read that it takes knowledge of about 1,500 words to be self-sufficient and get around, so that was my initial goal. In addition to that, I read for an additional 2-3 hours a night on material different than my class work. Don't have a Plan B to fall back on such as a translator, go all in but be organized about it. Develop a study schedule that includes vocabulary, reading, writing and speaking and stick to it. **Set short-term goals so you don't get overwhelmed.**

"You have to be smart. The easy days are over."

Robert Kiyosaki

START RISING

What has been one of your biggest challenges moving to a new country?

_____

_____

_____

_____

Are you doing all you can to adjust, including learning the language?

_____

_____

_____

_____

What are some short-term goals you still have?

_____

_____

_____

_____

Long-term goals?

_____

_____

_____

_____

Chapter Three

Community

We all develop groups of friendships based on interest as well as culture and language. For example, I started refereeing soccer for kids in the park near my home soon after high school and spent most Saturdays and Sundays out there encouraging the kids and talking with the parents. This was a natural for me since soccer has been a passion of mine for years. I started developing friendships with some of the parents as they became comfortable with me and grew to trust me.

Trust comes with time. Those parents saw me out there, treating their kids with respect and teaching them a great skill, week after week. Eventually, they no longer saw me as an outsider, I became part of that small group; I was one of them. When you become part of a circle, opportunities open up. We all look out for each other and share our lives with each other. Some people will be just casual, friendly acquaintances, and with others, there will be a deeper connection when you find you have more in common than just that one area.

Slowly, I started to develop more and more circles like this; I joined the Hispanic Chamber of Commerce and attended weekly meetings. I also joined a networking group that shared business opportunities within the group. The members would meet for breakfast once a week and get to know each other. Opportunities would only be shared when people trusted you. There was a saying in that group. **"Visibility, Credibility and Likeability"**, these were the steps needed to become a true member.

First, they needed to see you there, participating and working for the group. I would show up early and help get the room set up. I made myself visible. Credibility came with time as the trust developed that you were a person that would keep your word and do work as promised. Once they liked you, relationships developed, and opportunities were shared.

I saw many people come and go, thinking they could get a quick referral for a business opportunity without first taking those three steps. They left thinking they had wasted their time and money, never understanding that relationship was the essential link to success. Likability comes with following through and doing what you promised. People can only like you if they get to know you; relationships are what make the world go around! There is no shortcut to developing deep ties to your new community. It takes discipline, hard work and time. The rewards are profound, both personally and professionally.

But, even that is **not enough!** Those are the basics. If you really want to get ahead in your field or in life, you have to do more. In a job, for example, it's kind of expected that you are going to show up and do a great job - that's what you are getting paid to do. If you expect to get a raise or a promotion for just doing your job, you will be very disappointed. You have to add value above and beyond what is expected of you.

I would always do more than what I was getting paid for. This attitude of giving back more than you are getting applies to all things, not just work. In all my circles, I applied the same concept. I never expected to just take and not give back even more, whether in a community or business event, a job, or a new friendship. The thing about adding value to all you do is that it comes back to you tenfold. It's the old lesson that only by giving, will you truly receive. Do it without expecting anything in return. Do it because it's what you are supposed to do and it's the person you want to be. Being trustworthy and reliable is the low bar -- reach deeper.

Find a way to get involved with your community, church, business associations, non-profits, mastermind groups, chamber of commerce, etc. Whatever you do, be sure you enjoy it, get value from it, and provide value as well. It must be a win-win to be sustainable.

I find that I became a better person through the people that I met that were also trying to give back somehow. They inspired me to do better. I have made some of my best friends in my PCA (Porsche Club of America) group. These guys are solid -- some of the best people I have met, and I enjoy our time on and off the track.

Life is short and flies by so fast, why not spend it with people you enjoy and have something in common with? Always do what you can to improve the group and make it the best it can be. Some people get into a group just so they can be the center of attention, don't be that person! It's so rewarding to be a part of something bigger than yourself and give back without bragging. The satisfaction of helping the community is a reward in itself.

Giving back is not just about money, there is so much you can do for people in need. Sometimes they need a hand, or just a hug, or a shoulder to cry on. We currently have teacher programs where we give teachers supplies for their classrooms. We have a grant at the beginning of each semester that provides $1000 of material for the kids. Teachers apply for the program by writing a letter about what they would do with the money and how it could help the kids. It took on a life of its own as it grew and became more popular with over 100 applicant essays. It gives me such satisfaction when I hand that check to the teacher.

I started this program because I wanted to give to the community. I was not looking for a marketing angle, but the fact is, my name is associated with the program and it elevates our business in the community. It is definitely a win-win. The thing about giving to the community brings a level of satisfaction that is hard to describe. Those feelings overflow into all parts of my life.

Our teacher program began around 2016 and we are up to two teachers a year now. Start small and allow things to grow. Over time, more and more people donate to this cause. Don't wait too long to start what you want to do because you don't think it is large enough. It takes time for things to evolve and grow, much like a beautiful flower or a marvelous tree. Remember, one step at a time gets you to the top of the mountain. Start where you see a need and do what you can. Nurture it and watch it grow and evolve.

The ability to give back is an honor and really has nothing to do with the amount of money you make. It's about what's in your heart. There is no limit to the love you can carry in your heart and the more you give it away the stronger it is. I wonder what the world would be like if we could all give just a little to others in need. Please consider adding community work to your life, you will never regret it. I promise.

"To get the full value of joy you must have someone to divide it with."

Mark Twain

START RISING

Do you know people in your community who are making a difference? What are they doing that is helping change lives in a positive way?

_____

_____

_____

_____

What are you doing to contribute to your community?

_____

_____

_____

_____

What types of things are missing in your community that you can maybe help with?

_____

_____

_____

_____

Chapter Four

Education - formal or hard-knocks?

Formal education is not the answer for everyone. The government and the workforce teach you to get an education or a trade and then go to work for someone else. This is what keeps the business world running; they need employees, soldiers for the cause.

But, you may be one of those people that have the entrepreneurial spirit to develop your own business. For me, this is how I came to **"Rising in America."** I am writing this book to help those that want to fly with me. There is not just one way to get there. Many can get there by getting a college education and learning a trade. Others are reaching their goals through the school of "hard-knocks." I can't make that decision for you. If you are open to seeing your path, it will become clear over time, as long as you lay the foundation. There is really no such thing as luck, opportunities present themselves and you are either ready to jump on them or not.

The school of hard knocks is where people go out and learn on their own, without professional training or schooling. In the long run, it usually takes longer and costs more than getting a focused training, but it works for some people. I believe you should be smart and pay for some coaching, training, and/or a professional license. It might seem expensive at first, but believe me, it is far cheaper in the long run. We all need to also continue to do our own self-education; with books, audio tapes, YouTube videos, and many other methods. Some will be able to achieve the training or license they need to progress online, others may need a more formal, structured program.

The school of hard knocks as the sole means of study, is very hard and very expensive. My suggestion, and what has worked for me, is a combination of both. From there, it will depend on the subject that you are working on. Either way, you need to do it. It is going to be up to you to decide whether or not college or a university will serve your needs. There are professions out there that just need the credibility of that piece of paper before doors begin to open. Understand that college is the beginning of your education, not the end.

I see so many young kids, just out of high school, decide to go to college for the wrong reasons. They just get on the treadmill and go along with the crowd, never really giving it much thought. Maybe they want to get out of the house and party, or maybe their parents are pushing for them to go. Without a clue as to why they are going, they usually end up broke and in debt for the rest of their lives. It's so important to take your life into your own hands and make decisions about where you want to be and what you want to do.

I am suggesting that many people follow the path into college without thought and with no idea why. So, what is your why? If college is a means to an end, and you see your path - then that is the path to take. No one has a crystal ball to see how things will end up, but your chances of happiness are much greater if you pursue a dream you love instead of doing what you think you are supposed to do, or what everyone else thinks you should do.

"Rising in America" is not about making a personal fortune, it's about dreams. If you have a passion to become a scientist or any other field that requires an advanced degree, then go for it! I will be right there to cheer you on. Two of my daughters are currently in college, so I am not trying to discourage anyone from that path.

If you are not sure, that's ok. Sometimes it's necessary to do research, talk to people, or take a volunteer position prior to deciding on college. I have young kids coming into my business all the time, for a few weeks or a month, to get a feel for what it's like to work in the field. They are saving themselves a big, expensive headache by doing their homework. It's common for kids from European countries to take what they call a "gap year," where they travel or intern for the first year out of high school. It's the perfect time to do something like that before settling down and starting a career or family or studies. I think it's a great idea for many kids.

This is one of the most important times of your life, to set off in a certain direction and begin independence from family. Don't leave it up to someone else to decide what is best for you. No-one knows you better than you do! What do you like? What are your dreams and passions? What are you good at?

My path started with studies in Hotel/Restaurant Management right out of high school. I was also working in the industry at the same time in the field I was studying. I started at the Marriott my first year and through hard work, I was promoted four or five times to manager over a two-year period. I found myself hiring college students who were finishing their management degrees and my eyes were opened. Why would I finish two more years of school when I was already at a higher level than students finishing up? What would two more years of school give me that two years of more experience in the field wouldn't? Besides debt, that is. I had managed to pay my way up to that point and left college debt-free. I worked in that field for about five years as I continued to establish my networking and improve my language skills.

My work with the hotel industry led me naturally to real estate. I had family in that business in Brazil and always had an interest in it. I watched a friend of mine jump from the hospitality business to real estate and saw the success he was having; so, I made the jump in 2003. My people skills have been honed with my work over the years and I was a natural for this field.

With that said, one of the best business decisions I ever made was to work at the Marriott. I believe the training there was far superior to any I would have received in school As I rose up in the ranks, they had support and training for me. I learned how to run entire departments and always was given the understanding of how the whole structure worked. I use all of the skills I learned at the Marriott in my businesses today. My Ritz Carlton excellence training is by far a unique value proposition of mine.

The other great business decision I made was leaving the Marriott and taking a leap of faith. For me, having those skills under my belt saved me years of struggle and propelled me toward success. I would not have been able to do it without the foundation that was formed in my prior work experiences.

In 2010, I bought into my first ReMax Franchise, and by 2016, I opened my second franchise with my partner, Mario Negron. We started with less than 10 agents and currently have almost thirty. I am also a team leader to the Houston New Home Team which is considered # 3 in Houston by the *Houston Business Journal* and have been in the top ten in Texas for the last five years with more than $80 million dollars in production annually. I've helped over 2000 families find a home over the last nine years.

The self-education had never stopped and I turned my energy to my new profession and continued my studies. There is always more to learn. Some think that the piece of paper you are bestowed at graduation from college is the end of learning, but they will be surprised and disappointed when they sit back and expect to be a success. I will never stop learning and striving to improve myself and my businesses. It is challenging, fun, and rewarding.

"Formal education will make you a living and self-education will make you a fortune."

Jim Rohn

START RISING

What are your formal educational and training goals?

_____

_____

_____

_____

What are some of your informal educational goals?

_____

_____

_____

_____

What types of learning activities can you take on your own to improve your potential?

_____

_____

_____

_____

Chapter Five

Self-Employment or Employment?

So, this is where it gets tricky. Self-employment isn't for everyone. It depends on your learning style and how self-motivated you are. You have to take a hard look in the mirror and be honest. Do you learn well on your own? If not, then a class or designed program would be best for you to help you with learning a new skill. Or maybe you need to develop the skills needed to be more self-sufficient such as time-management and good habit development. In that case, you may be able to find a coach or an online class that can help you see what is needed to be self-employed. Remember 50% of all small businesses fail in the first five years. Are you prepared for the consequences of failure? What makes you think you are in the top 50%?

There is really no "right" answer here. There are always pros and cons to all decisions, and this is no exception. Many people romanticize self-employment. They will say things like, "You are so lucky to be self-employed; you can take time off whenever you want," or they assume anyone who has their own business in rolling in the dough. The reality is much different -- working long hours, sometimes not being able to pay yourself, or even worse, working hard all week and needing to pay the business to stay open that week. It can be tough to get a small business off the ground.

The consequences of failure can also be daunting. If you are like most people, you will have to take out a loan to start a business. What happens if it fails? If you want to quit a regular job, you give your notice and start printing up your resumes. If you fail at a small business, there are usually still bills to pay. It is not something that can simply be walked away from like a regular job can.

When you start up your own business, you are usually wearing all the hats throughout the day. There is marketing to do, then finances, then negotiating contracts, hiring and training staff and on and on. It always seems impossible to be able to afford the next step until you can make enough to invest back in.

If it is a one-person operation, and you are that person, things can get lonely and motivation can start to dissipate. If you have partners, there is going to invariably be conflicts and disagreements to work out. Having a business partner can feel a lot like having a marriage. You will spend many hours of many days with that person, seeing and hearing all their fears and worries as well as the good stuff too. It is a rare person that can maintain the relationship needed for a partnership to succeed as well as having the friendship still intact.

There are other options besides a start-up that help with the risk. If you are able to buy into a franchise or even buy an established small business, there will be a financial history there that allows you a better understanding of the profit. There are regular customers, employees that are already trained and systems in place. But, there will be a price to pay for all of that.

Still, the allure of being your own boss is real. The ability to be able to conceive of and grow a small business from the beginning – it's no wonder so many entrepreneurs call their small business their "baby!" The pride of ownership and the satisfaction of being the best you can be without answering to anyone is hard to beat.

The potential for making it big is also very real. Not only can you make a lot of money owning your own business, you can often turn around and sell it when you are ready to move to your next adventure. A successful business can really change your life and allow you to afford a great lifestyle even after leaving it.

Of course, I have talked to self-employed people who pine for the steady paycheck employment offers, not to mention the 8-hour days, the insurance benefits and more. Mostly they wish they could leave their job at work sometimes and just go home. Starting a new business usually involves being available for questions at all hours of the day and night.

If you are considering buying or opening a business, you have to be prepared for friends and family to try to talk you out of it. It is just a natural tendency for people to discourage those who want to go out on their own. Maybe it's because many folks try to go out there unprepared to really run a business. It's so much more than getting a business loan and hanging your shingle.

Maybe there is a lot of cynicism because people have made choices to stay in a "safe" job, thinking it was the best thing for their family's future. There might be a part of them that does not want to see someone take the risks they wished they had taken.

So many people sit in a job they hate, making just enough money to scrape by and they count the days until they can retire. Who knows how long we all have? I cannot imagine spending my life doing something I hate. This is not what God gave us our life for! I believe we need to find our full potential and live it. **There is no "safe" job anymore.** Companies lay people off, they go out of business, and pensions are a rare commodity now. This is a different world

44

than many Americans think. One the thing that holds true --
America provides an opportunity to soar whether self-
employed or employed.

It always comes back to the same equation. Measure
out your pros and cons and make the best decision you can
make. Do it without fear being a factor. There are so many
things that "could" happen, all we know for sure is that
"something" will happen. Finding happiness and satisfaction in
your chosen profession is not something you want to leave up
to chance or to someone else. This is one you really need to
work out for yourself.

So, the number one reason I jumped out of a solid job
with security into being self-employed was that the potential
earnings had no natural cap on them. Nothing could stop me
from growing except my own limitations. At the Marriott, there
was security, but I had started to hit the ceiling as far as pay.
A business is not going to continue to increase salaries
indefinitely. This is the key difference between being self-
employed and being an employee of a large system. They
have a place for you, and it will seldom be at the top.

When I gave my notice at the Marriott, my manager
was so surprised, "You have so much potential!" he said. I
said, "I know, that's why I'm leaving." I never looked back. I
had done my homework and knew what it would take to be a
success; it was a well-thought-out calculation. I also knew it

was going to take commitment and hard work to achieve my goals.

"If you aim at nothing, you will hit it every time."

Zig Zigler

START RISING

For you, personally, what would be the advantages of being employed?

_____

_____

_____

_____

Self-employed?

_____

_____

_____

_____

At this time in your life, are you happy with your employment status? Why or why not?

_____

_____

_____

_____

Are there any changes you might need to make?

_____

_____

_____

_____

Chapter Six

Personal Development

Life-long learning comes in many forms but it is a must. I have logged thousands of hours of audio tapes, eBooks and videos to help keep me focused on my goals. I spend a lot of time driving, so it was a no-brainer to start doing this in the car. In fact, I started educating myself about self-employment long before I had my own business. I remember learning that the company you currently work for is your best client at the moment and will be one of many. You need to treat your job as if you were self-employed and they are **your best client**. Treat them like they are the most important client you have. If nothing else, it helps to train your mind to accept the changes to come.

Back in 2004, I invested in an audio class that was put on by Jim Rohn. It was 36 CDs and it had a strong influence on me. It was insane! I listened to that seminar for about 2 ½ years and it helped me make the jump. Brian Tracy was also an influence on me. He was very precise and not overly animated, but his information was powerful.

Sometimes, one sentence or phase can change your entire outlook and frame your actions in the future. It's important to seek out mentors that speak to your heart and help focus your thoughts in a positive way. For example, I learned that you have to be part of what is happening every day in your business. As you begin to grow, it is easy to lose touch with the basics. That reminder caused me to routinely have lunch with my realtors and employees to check in and see what was on their minds.

Personal Development is about more than professional studies though. If that is all you did, your life would be pretty boring! We've all met that guy at the party who drones on and on about his job. Don't be that person! It's important to expand your horizons and learn new things. One of the best ways of doing this is by reading. Read about anything that interests you other than your job. History, astronomy, art, you name it! The library is full of books and reading is also a great way to continue to expand your vocabulary.

Just like in the professional part of your life, you have to grow and develop yourself personally as well. Many people do lots of training and development on their professional life but do nothing or very little on his or her personal life.

Look for progress every day and maintain habits that support your goals. I look at four areas of my life to focus on daily. If you neglect any one of the areas, you will not be able to sustain a happy, healthy lifestyle. They are your physical self, professional life, family life, and your personal relationship with yourself.

First, you have to take care of your physical body. If you are not exercising, eating well and getting the sleep you need, you will not be at full capacity. This is critical. Health is more than physical however; the mental and spiritual side of things is tied into your physical body as well. If you are not well mentally or spiritually, you can become physically ill and the opposite is true as well. For example, if you are suffering from anxiety that is affecting your ability to sleep, you will not be in peak physical condition.

You could start by reading about natural health or exercise if you have neglected the physical side of health. Educating yourself about health can help with understanding where to begin. For example, if you find you eat out all the time at fast-food restaurants, it might be fun and helpful to take a cooking class or read a good cookbook and try some new recipes.

People don't think they have the time to give to their personal health, but they are only kicking the ball down the

52

road. This will catch up to you. But in order to take on exercise, it needs to be convenient and fun. So, spend some time and figure out what's going to work for you. Some people love to get up early and start the day with exercise like yoga or running, others like to go to the gym after work and release the stress of the day. It's funny that exercise also helps with stress as well, so if you exercise, you will feel better physically as well as mentally. What do you do to keep your body healthy?

The wonderful thing about the body is that it is generally very forgiving and will naturally heal and grow stronger if you get the obstacles out of its way. Once you start taking the small steps towards better health, you will start to feel changes very soon. You are either getting healthier or getting sicker; the body is not a stagnant object. Which path are you walking down now, towards health or towards disease?

You have the power to make that choice. It starts, like any change, with a small step. Decide to eat more vegetables today, or take a break from your desk and walk for 15 minutes. Take a small step towards improving your health and that step can lead you to a new exciting life.

I am not a person who enjoys working out in a gym, I know that about myself. So, I do what I enjoy, jogging, biking and muscling high speed cars around the track. This can definitely work up a sweat! Find what exercise or activity you love to do and figure out a way to incorporate it into your daily life. Move your body or it will forget how!

Don't ever make the mistake of neglecting your family or thinking they don't need your personal attention every day. They are everything! It is easy to take the people in your life for granted, it seems they are always there for you, but then suddenly they may not be. If you don't have 15 minutes to check in with your kids every day, then something is wrong in your life. Give them the encouragement to face their day, life is not so easy for kids these days! Do you know what is going on in your children's lives?

What about your spouse? When is the last time you did something special and unexpected for him or her? Treasure and nourish your relationship, don't expect it to run on remote control. It's the little things that matter. For example, my wife and I have dinner together every night. It's our time to talk about our days and spend special time together. This is what success is all about! We both work hard and look forward to our time together. At the end of dinner, it seems our heads are clear of worries and we don't have to lay awake thinking about stressful things, as they have been all talked out. We don't only talk about worries! We plan, talk about our kids, and about our dreams.

The happiness of your spouse is just as important as your own, we are a team! My wife is much more outgoing and extroverted than I am, she is always up and lively and ready to go to a party or have some friends over. I'm more of an introvert, so she gets me out of my comfort zone, which is a good thing. I get her to be more organized and focused at times, and it works for us. I don't think I would have learned how to come home from work if my wife hadn't been there!

We bought a house in 2008 and my wife wanted a pool, I told her we should not put the pool in unless we pay for it in cash. I would save for half for the pool and she would save for the other half. After two years we put our pool savings together in order to build our dream pool. My wife cried from the pride she felt at reaching that goal and contributing to the home. We look at all of our decisions together as a team and it brings us closer.

When we wanted to get a beach house, we did the same thing. We looked at the budget and together we saved to make it a reality. After two and a half years of saving, we were able to buy a beach house right on the water in Gulf of Mexico.

It seems there are some many people that are not happy in their marriages or don't have a good relationship with their kids. No relationship is perfect, but most can be healed. If you are having trouble in your relationships, seek out some help. Sometimes it can be as easy as starting a conversation. Do you take the time to sit down with your spouse or your kids if there seems to be resentment, and ask them how they are feeling? Of course, it is not that simple most of the time, but you have to start somewhere, right?

I find that most people that are unhappy with their marriage or their kids would still be unhappy if they were single and childless. They are unhappy with themselves; the kids and the spouse are just their excuse not to look at themselves and their actions. This is a tough habit to change but it can be done. I do believe that unhappiness can sometimes just be a lifelong habit of looking at the negative side of things. This habit can be changed the same way physical habits are changed, one step at a time.

Start by taking the time to check in with yourself every day. Some people do this by keeping a daily journal, others may take 15 minutes to meditate every day. Whatever it is, make sure you are in touch with your feelings and love yourself! This is one that is so easy to ignore! We all know that person that does for everyone else but never for themselves. They will eventually burn out. I do what I call, **"feed the king!"** In order to be better for anyone, you have to be better for yourself. You will be a better boss, a better husband, son, and employee, if you take care of yourself first. I look at myself every day and I talk to myself every day, if I can't stand myself who will? You need to love yourself.

If you have trouble understanding yourself, I would recommend starting with astrology. Even as a kid, I would read about my sign and try to see how true it was. I'm a

Capricorn and many of the things I see or hear about Capricorns holds true for me. For example, I am ambitious, persistent, practical, and disciplined. Some would also say stubborn... well I am that too! My wife is a Leo, charismatic, majestic, giving, and honest. We work well together because we don't deny who we are, we work with our strengths and weaknesses, and recognize there is good and bad in them all.

Astrology gives some clues and helps you get a sense of who you are. You can also go to family members and ask them their memories of you as a young kid. Ask them what your personality was like, how they felt about you -- any memories they want to share! Usually, that is easier than asking them how they feel about you now. They will project your adult life onto your childhood and tell you exactly how they feel about you now! It will be insightful without being offensive.

I know people that are in their 40s and are just starting to look under the hood to see where they might have gone wrong. They have never considered there might be an issue with the way they treat people or the way they deal with conflict until they found themselves divorced and lonely. It was always someone else's fault. It's important to try to see yourself for who you are and to make the changes you have to while you are still young and have your life ahead of you. Don't let pride or old resentments or fears stop you from finding happiness. Some people can never admit they made a mistake or contributed in any way to even a small stupid argument. These are not characteristics that are desirable in a work environment or a marriage. It's the reason people find themselves fired from a job or divorced with no clue of what happened. Instead, they blame it all on everyone else.

It's important to take time for yourself, shut off the cell phone and the computer, and just re-group. I do this by reading, watching a movie by myself, or going for a drive. A good friend of mine recently had a panic attack that came out of nowhere. When I talked to him about it later, I asked him if he was under any stress, he said, "No, I don't have any stress!" Of course, that is impossible, we all have stress. The more we talked, the more all the things he had on his plate came out. He had been juggling many stressful things and never giving himself a chance to put them down and take a break for himself.

If you do the work you need to do on yourself, you will learn that you are not perfect, **you are human**, just like the rest of us. You make mistakes and get tired and cranky, and you need to learn to say you are sorry sometimes -- it's not that hard! Save yourself a lot of heartache and get to know yourself and what makes you tick. I know for example, that I love cars and that is a place I can go for relaxation and stress reduction.

I especially love racing cars and I have made a point to carve out time for my passion for cars. This thing I do for myself improves my relationship with family while keeping me happy. I started collecting and racing cars about six years ago.

Now I do endurance racing, sprint racing, time trials, and more. I am a PCA club instructor, so I also teach people how to do high-speed driving. I own multiple race cars and love them all! I personally love adrenaline, so I enjoy chasing that extra second and analyzing how I can push it more.

Next, you must tend to the professional side of your life. If you are just on remote control and get up and go to work every day without thought or without a plan, you will not progress or be satisfied in your work. Be your best every day, but be you. Don't waste your time worrying about what others think of you -- they are not focusing on themselves if they are focusing on you. Do your work and do it the best you can. Bring your whole self to work. Once you are there, give it everything.

Each day, I make a point of checking in on each of these areas to see how I can improve myself and my actions. Having the structure in place that easily allows me to review the four foundational aspects of life helps prevent any one thing from getting out of hand. I am constantly checking in and considering my actions in relation to my family, my health, my profession, and myself.

"Never wish life were easier, wish that you were better. "

Jim Rohn

START RISING

What types of personal development activities have you tried in the past?

_____

_____

_____

_____

How do you check in with yourself when it comes to your health?

_____

_____

_____

_____

Your family?

_____

_____

_____

_____

Your profession?

_____

_____

_____

_____

Your personal happiness?

_____

_____

_____

_____

Chapter Six

Work Ethics and Strategy

I believe that a **strong work ethic** can be taught. When I start with a new agent, I tell them that no-one is going to come knocking on their door to tell them that they've won the lottery. They have to work hard. That is the formula. Working smart comes after the hard work and it never replaces it. You cannot just work smart and not work hard as well. Nothing is going to be given to you, you have to earn it.

When I hire a new agent, I base it on attitude more than experience. Most of us can be trained if we have the desire to learn. Loyalty and a willingness to learn is so critical. One person on the team with an attitude really can change the entire team dynamic. When you are out there looking for a job, be sure to express your desire to learn from the company and to be available.

We are in a country of abundance. When you come from somewhere where things are more scarce, and you may have to fight with dozens of other people to get that one thing that here, in America, you can just go to the grocery store to pick up, it creates a different perspective on life. Do immigrants have a tougher work ethic? Maybe. I sometimes see it in other immigrants, and I've had people comment to me that they think immigrants have a better work ethic than many Americans who were born here.

Does excess breed laziness? In other countries, you don't see things like "garage sales," where literal junk is being sold. You don't have storage units because you've accumulated so much stuff it doesn't fit in your house anymore. What does that excess do to a society? I think sometimes if things come to you easily, including things and stuff, you don't appreciate it as much as something that you worked very hard for.

Where I came from, for example, if you came to school and didn't have lunch, you needed to get in line for that lunch. If you got in at the end of the line, there would be no food for you. That doesn't happen in the United States. Even the poorest kids, if they get in line, they get their lunch. The food doesn't "run out," like it might in some other countries or cultures.

So, when you live through that, you realize that you have to hustle to get your share. You don't have to necessarily push people out of the way, you just have to make sure you are where you need to be, literally and figuratively, to get your share. Is this the basis for a positive immigrant work ethic? I feel like, at times, when I'm looking to get something done, or achieve something, I know I need to get ready and be prepared for whatever comes my way. I'm not sure if I would have figured that out at a young age, had I not been an immigrant to this country.

Stop looking for the easy out and start planning your journey. Where do you want to be? What do you want to do? How are you planning on giving back? All of these questions need to stay in the front of your mind and help keep you focused on your goals. Go to work and work hard! Show up early, stay later. Be the go-to person for your boss, learn from everyone and everything. Be a sponge, take and take and take.

The knowledge you acquire and the experiences you live are the tools you need to do better and become better. The money will come once you become worthy of it. For life to happen, you must make it happen first!

Be friendly with all your co-workers but stay away from "that" group of people. You know which one -- the copier bunch, smokers crowd, whichever one is the gossiping bunch. There is no reason to get caught up in the drama that is in every workplace. If someone tries to engage with gossip, politely change the subject and get back to work. Stay above the fray!

Doing a good job and helping others when you can is the best remedy to avoiding workplace drama. Gossip is a hobby for people that don't have any passion for their work, so they create drama to make their lives more interesting… to them at least. If you do not take the bait, they will eventually figure out that you are the person that cares about the business and about work. They may even start to seek you out for advice.

Stay focused on how to improve the work you do. Take small steps, one at a time. Look for progress not perfection. It's easy to get burned out if you try to shoot too big at one time. It's like when I focused on learning 10 to 20 words a week. I didn't try to learn the whole language at once! I set goals that were realistic and I focused on them. Day by day, week by week, I moved forward. It is a journey not a marathon. Whether it's in the gym, doing one more rep, or staying 30 minutes later at work, stay focused on the steps that are leading you to your destination.

I was recently watching a *Rocky* movie where he was talking to Adonis Creek, and for some reason, it moved me. He said, "One step at a time. One punch at a time. One round at a time." That is a great mantra for life. Don't try to do everything at once. Stay focused on the task at hand and keep moving forward. Go back to the basics.

One of my personal struggles has been *procrastination*. It is something I recognize and so I can nip it in the bud when I see it. I know that this is a natural occurrence, but it is always hard to acknowledge your **weaknesses**. I think finding your weaknesses is as important as understanding your strengths.

Statistics have always been a part of all aspects in my life. It is just information, like a budget, but it seems to terrify some people. It's not for where you are, it's where you are going. I look at it as a way to show me where I need to focus. So many businesses skip on the data because they get so caught up on the day-to-day of keeping the doors open, that they never take the time to look at the numbers and analyze them.

I believe that just taking the time to look at the stats of your business starts to improve them even before acting on them -- they are that powerful. Once you can see, on paper, where you are with your numbers, the path forward is so much clearer.

I take this belief with me into my hobbies as well. I am competitive by nature and I like to compete with myself as well! So, I know my racing speeds, how quickly I am taking the corners, etc. This allows me to constantly try to improve and also set goals. Once a goal is reached, then it's fun to give yourself a reward.

This could be a simple thing like a trip to Starbucks or a special chocolate treat (my favorite)! Or, if a massive landmark goal has been reached, it might be something much better. The reward is important because it keeps you motivated and focused on your goals.

I have an end-of-month routine with my wife where we celebrate the month and acknowledge it. This may be in the form of a special night out or maybe a weekend away. The important thing is to celebrate the steps along the way and to reward yourself when you hit a goal, big or small.

I am a big believer in incentives and rewards in my business as well, for motivation and team cohesiveness. I consider my company a second family and I love to show my support for them with encouragement and challenge rather than criticism. The reward must be meaningful; that is more important than the cost. I have taken the whole team on a cruise together, including spouses. I also acknowledge birthdays with a collage of images from the year on a cube that they can put on their desks. This is more of a sentimental gift than an expensive one, but the point is to care about your employees and show them.

I applied the same principles to learning high-speed driving as I do to my business. I set goals for myself, but took small steps to achieve them. I hired a coach when needed and studied online as well as attending many workshops and races. I never stop reading and learning about racing cars. When I got my first car, a 911 turbo, rear-engine Porsche, I realized I needed to learn how to drive it! So that started me down the road to racing.

For those that are interested, I have owned multiple cars over the years from muscle cars to exotics, cars such as Camaro, Mustangs, Mercedes Benz, BMWs, multiple Porsches, Ferrari, and a 2018 Lamborghini Performante which can accelerate from 0 to 100 mph in 5.6 seconds and is rated for a top speed of approximately 202 mph. I've also owned a few race cars, including a SR8 Radical Sportscar, which is a British race car, and my Houston "must have," a F-250 Monster Truck.

The feeling I get behind the wheel is a joy that is hard to describe. There is the challenge and the desire to improve, but also, I get a real Zen when I am in the zone and racing along. All my worries are gone, and I am focusing on what is right in front of me -- the track. It is pure pleasure, no fear, just fun. The next day when I go back to work, my brain is fresh and ready to start the day.

Even the smallest rewards stimulate the endorphins and re-enforce the motivation to continue to improve your performance. Don't get caught up in the expense of the reward, do something you desire at the moment. The important thing is to acknowledge your progress in a meaningful way.

In the office, we have created a partnership of work ethics. Basically, we all hold each other accountable for being on time, working hard, being at open houses, supporting the efforts of others in the office, and working together as a team. Another aspect of our work ethic at the office, and in my own personal life, is to work in service. I am in service to my family, to my colleagues, and to my clients. Our agents at the office are in service to their clients and vendors -- we do not push and push and push like a hardcore salesperson might. Our job is to be of service, and to work hard for people, building rapport and even friendships.

"True happiness and fulfillment are found within myself,
every day - today, not tomorrow."

Alex Rezende

START RISING

How do you define your personal work ethic?

_____

_____

_____

_____

What do you do when you see people compromise their ethics?

_____

_____

_____

_____

How do you model positive ethics and morals to those around you?

_____

_____

_____

_____

Chapter Seven

Roots

As an immigrant, you will always have a strong bond to your native country, it's part of who you are and what you represent. It influences every aspect of your life. Religion, politics and other beliefs are things that you grow up with from an early age, and they will always be with you in some way. Assimilating into this country does not mean giving up your roots! I am so proud to be Brazilian and I love my hometown and country and proudly represent my people. I also love and represent the USA. I am blessed to have two amazing places to live. I am not less Brazilian than when I lived in Brazil.

Think of it like divorced parents, you can still love them both and if they get remarried, there is room in your heart to love your new step-parent as well. The fact is that you want to grow to be the best you. Over time, you will be a different person, but always be your authentic self. Never be afraid to show your pride in your roots. It's what makes America great. This amazing country was founded on the principle that immigrants can **come together** and become stronger because of their differences. If you have a huge heart, there is always room for one more. Brazil and America both hold special places in my heart and have given me so much, making me the man I am today. I am welcome in both places and can come and go as I please. I love having two countries to call home.

Anything I do to improve me, is good for both countries. I can help and do more for both than I could many years back. I am so proud to be able to contribute to the wellbeing of my communities in both countries and be a positive influence in people's lives. I care deeply about my friends and family back in Brazil and keep the connects strong.

One of the traits that I have maintained from my upbringing is my strong Christian faith, which influences all my actions. I love that this country fosters faith without forcing a belief on anyone; this is my understanding of religion as well -- it is a personal choice. When Hurricane Harvey hit our community, it was just understood in our family that we would help our neighbors in any way we could, this is just what you do in a time of need. This is part of my faith and is what was instilled in me as a small child in Brazil.

Of course, I have changed over time and transform into a different person; we all evolve and change. This is normal

74

and does not mean you love your home country any less. It's necessary to adapt and change in your new country. The important thing is to change to make yourself a better person today than you were yesterday. Only then can you continue to help those you come in contact with. I try to learn something new from every person I meet. Learning comes from many places.

Take the strengths from your past and your heritage and hold onto them. Even if they are not serving you at the moment, they are priceless. For example, being bilingual allows me the freedom of travel in many countries. I have the added benefit of learning enough Spanish in high school to get around in Spanish-speaking countries as well. Travel is a great way to expand your understanding of the world and of people. Through travel I also find many unexpected opportunities can present themselves. As an immigrant, you are going to be bilingual once you master English and this is a very useful skill to have. It will serve you well over the years.

Everything that has happened to you, all of your experiences, skills, friendships, etc, they are all valuable in getting you to where you are and where you want to go. I can't tell you how often an old friend would be a source of information, support or knowledge that helped propel me past an obstacle. You just never know who you may meet or what they may have that can help you down the road. I treat everyone I meet with respect and consideration -- that is just who I am – you never know when that person you just met will change your life!

Once, when I was still in the hotel industry, I was working the front desk as I was short-staffed that weekend. As the front office supervisor, I sometimes needed to step into that role and do check-ins, etc. A man walked in and asked about meeting spaces and function rooms for his company. I took the time to show him around the hotel and talked about the services we could provide. The next day I was called into the sales office and told that the gentleman I showed around was the CEO of a large company building nearby and he had purchased 100 rooms for two years; his contract was upwards of 50 million dollars! Well, that day I was promoted to sales and received a large bonus! Don't make assumptions about people you meet; you never know who they really are until you get to know them as a person.

No one does this alone. Do not be a person who burns bridges. As you go through different experiences and develop friendships, everything starts to weave into a web of support that can catch you when you fall. We all lift each other up and become stronger through our connections.

"Your next step is your first step into your future!"

Alex Rezende

START RISING

Describe a time when you might have inadvertently burned a bridge.

_____

_____

_____

_____

What would you do differently if you could?

_____

_____

_____

_____

How do your roots define you?

_____

_____

_____

_____

Chapter Eight

Judging People

People tend to automatically **judge** what they do not understand. This happens all the time when a person comes to the country and has trouble with the language. There may be an assumption that a person who is learning the language will always be at the level they are when they first get here. That is simply not the case. The vast majority of immigrants strive to learn the language and fit in. In fact, the third generation from a family that came to this country has usually lost the ability to speak the home country's language.

There are also people born in this country who never learn English. I knew a friend whose grandmother was born in Vermont and spoke French her entire life. Her children were bilingual and her grandkids couldn't speak a word of French. Just because someone is bilingual or speaks another language does not mean they were not born here. I also know a friend who was never asked for her "papers" at the various checkpoints in AZ that are looking for undocumented people. These checkpoints are up to 100 miles from the border and many Hispanic people will have their papers ready because they are asked so often. This woman was from Canada and went through the checkpoint weekly. She was not a citizen, but did have a work visa.

I know that assumptions are made every day based on looks, clothes, the cars people drive, and the way they talk. I train my employees and agents to treat everyone with respect and make no assumptions about their ability to buy a home.

Take the time to get to know people and they will surprise you. It can happen both ways - someone may come into the office looking for a high-end house only to be turned away due to credit issues. I remember one couple who had moved to Houston from Florida, just so they could get an affordable house. The wife worked for McDonalds and the husband worked at Walmart. They had one child and had never owned a home, but their credit was impeccable. I was able to get them into a $119,000 home with 3 bedrooms and one bath. They were thrilled to have achieved their dream of homeownership.

Think about how long they must have planned and worked for that goal. I know they did the research needed to see where they could afford to buy and then took the steps necessary to get transferred in their respective jobs out here. I felt blessed to be part of this process with them, this has happened to me so many times. We are a blessing to each other.

At the same time, as you achieve success, you may be the subject of judgment as well. When this happens to me, I tend to analyze it to figure out whether or not it is a legitimate judgment or criticism, or is it someone just talking down about me to make me feel bad? Judgment is a part of life. It's easy to write off a judgment that someone makes about you, because it can feel like an insult. Sometimes I just ignore a negative judgment or criticism, especially if there's really no basis in truth for it.

But, part of being an immigrant, and an American, is owning up to who you are, for better or worse. It's not enough to brush off negative thoughts without any further reflection. It's quite possible that someone's negative judgment of you has some truth to it, and in that case you should take a look in the mirror, let your ego down, and see what it is that you can improve in your life.

With that said, there are people who constantly judge, and it's because **they are reflecting their own negative thoughts about themselves onto others.** Think of the classic bully at school. More often than not, they are bullied at home, so they are taking it out on others. When you choose who to surround yourself with, don't choose bullies. For example, at our office, we make sure that we are only hiring and working people who have a positive self-image, and who treat others in a positive way. That creates a very functional and productive environment to work in.

We have no room for negativity at our office. Likewise, I don't at home, either. It's up to each of us to stop negativity in its tracks and shift the gears or focus so that we can now see the positive. I believe that negativity is energy, just like being positive is energy. Negative energy depletes positive energy, and it's contagious. You've seen it -- someone enters a room or a setting where things are positive, but they're very negative. All of a sudden, others join them in noticing the negative.

The best thing you can do is strike negativity from your life. I think this is where most judgement comes from, as it's usually negative in nature. For instance, at our real estate office, I've had to ask agents to leave. I always give them a chance and talk to them if I sense that their attitude is negative. But, if they don't change, if they don't turn that energy around, I have no problem asking them to go. Life and work are tough enough as it is, sometimes; there's no need for a negative person to drag you, or anyone you care about, down.

At the same time, as I talked about above, it's important to look deeper than the surface. We had one agent, for example, who was really creating a negative vibe in the office. People were starting to come to me, complaining about this woman, and how destructive her attitude was becoming in the office. I knew that I needed to talk with her, sooner than later.

I called her into my office and sat her down across from me and made a point to not sit behind my desk. She and I sat as equals having a conversation. I started gently, "Alice, is there something going on? You seem really negative lately, and we're concerned. Not just about you, but also how it's affecting our culture here."

She broke into tears, and told me of what was going on in her life, which was basically some pretty intense family drama.

Now, she had worked with us for long enough that I knew this negative attitude was not her normal state of being. So, I felt like we could work with her.

"Listen," I said, "This isn't you -- it's just what you're going through right now. This isn't normally how you are, it's just the situation you're going through right now. So, how can we help you out? What kind of time do you need to take for yourself?"

It was a simple, easy, and gentle conversation that not only sent a message that we cared about her, but that we also needed to protect the positive culture that we had worked so hard to grow. We didn't want to judge her attitude by just looking on the surface. We wanted to help her understand how she was creating something negative, but we could also see how it was due to some really difficult things going on in her life.

After that talk, and Alice taking a couple days to get things in order at home, she came back to the office, to our welcome arms. By withholding judgment about Alice, and being patient and understanding, we were able to preserve our positive working and office culture. In our office, we are all here for each other, and that's what helped Alice so much. In fact, I don't think people would have complained about Alice's attitude if we didn't have a caring culture. They were concerned about keeping our work family happy and feeling emotionally safe, so they spoke up. As hard as it was for Alice to hear that some of her colleagues were expressing concern about her attitude, she realized that they spoke up because they cared so much for what we were creating together, and cared about the individual, as well.

It's critical to create a positive culture no matter where you are. In your home, at the office, among friends, in volunteer organizations. There's not enough time in the day to get good work done, and to help people out. It's a waste of that limited time to be making judgments, excluding people, or bringing people down. As an immigrant, I try to make sure that my interactions with everyone around me reflect positively on my Brazilian culture, as well as my new American culture.

"Most everything that you want is just outside your comfort."

Jack Canfield

START RISING

How have you been judged negatively in the past?

_____

_____

_____

_____

Can you think of a time when you judged someone unfairly?

_____

_____

_____

_____

What would you do differently in that case?

_____

_____

_____

_____

Chapter Nine

Success

I do not see money as the key to success. I have many friends back in Brazil that have very little in the way of finances or possessions, yet they are remarkably happy with their lives. I also see so many people here in the U.S. with more than they could ever use or spend, and they are always looking outside of themselves to find happiness. So, who is the more successful of the two? I think the answer is obvious if you measure success in terms of happiness. I have only met one man in my life who said his goal was to be rich, not happy. He wasn't either in the end! His wife divorced his miserable self and got the home and the bank account!

Success for me is having a wonderful family and being able to live a life I have dreamed of. It's having the best friends I could ask for. Success is loving myself and enjoying every day. It's learning from the experiences I have had, good and bad. Success is spending time and money on adventures and special events, not things.

I learned a long time ago not to chase money. It's easy to get caught up in the "image" of success, but there is no reason to try to "keep up with the Joneses." You will only find yourself with a bunch of new, expensive toys you really don't want and a pile of debt.

Chase your passions instead, do what you are good at, and what you enjoy. Be smart about it and do the research, make your plans, and take it one step at a time. Be you, do you, there is only one you! Success is not about having things so much as it is about being me.

Expectations are part of the equation, if you buy into the idea that bigger is better, you may be disappointed if you don't get what you think you need. We don't really need much, a roof over our heads, food on the table, someone to share it with, a sense of self-worth and value in the community. What more do we really need? **Happiness comes from within, not from what you have.**

Part of success is establishing balance in your life. If everything you do revolves around work, that will eventually break down. My kids love to see me, but only for about 5-10 minutes now that they are teenagers! But when they were kids, I spent more like two hours a day with them. I do not maintain a rigid schedule with family and friends, but I check in and spend time as it is needed with my wife and kids. If there is a friend in need, I always try to be there for them.

I do have a morning ritual that allows me to maintain the balance needed in my life. I start with meditation. I check in with myself and my emotions to see if there is anything that may need addressing before I start my day.

What is the point of having a great business if your home life is a wreck? Your problems will always follow you to work and drag you down if they are not resolved. If there is an agent in the office who is living beyond his means and desperate for a sale, it shows, and it scares people off. They can sense that he is not there for them, but only for himself. Your mind has to be clear when you are serving your clients, and you always act in their best interest.

Vacation is a good example. I sometimes have to force people to take time off for themselves. If my team doesn't have balance in their lives, it will eventually start to affect my business as well. It's a win-win if everyone has the energy to give to the company without feeling overwhelmed with stress.

I visited the Biltmore Estate recently, which is considered the largest house built in the United States. It's a museum now, though still privately owned. I love looking at houses so I wanted to see this. George Vanderbilt had it built in 1889, he called this summer home, his "little mountain escape." It is a 125,000 sq. ft home which is currently housed on 8,000 acres, though the estate was much larger at one time.

The great irony of the Biltmore is that when George died suddenly in 1914, his widow, Ethel was then burdened with the task of maintaining this property. She lived in an apartment that was in a section of the former "Bachelor's Wing," who really needs more? It was an overwhelming task for her to manage the house, not to mention that it was very expensive. The family opened it to the public for a time during the Great Depression in an attempt to improve the estate's financial situation. It became profitable only in the late 1950's. Currently, it receives over 1.4 million visitors a year.

I left my visit to the Biltmore wondering if Ethel felt "successful" as she struggled with all the wealth her husband had left her. What about George? He was certainly a success in terms of consolidating wealth and leaving a legacy, but was he happy in his life? He may have been very happy, chasing his dreams, I have no idea.

What I do know is that success is personal for each person, **but it all boils down to being true to yourself**, whatever that may look like.

We are currently number three in the Houston market. There are people in my field that assume I am naturally striving to be number one, but they are mistaken. I look at the tactics and strategies that some firms take to become number one, and I know that is not who I am. This is not true only in the real estate business, but in all businesses. If clients are not your first concern, then there are ways to increase profit margins, often at the expense of the client. I would rather be the best number three I can be and deliver excellent service to those who walk through my door, than sacrifice my morals to become number one.

To be true to myself, I learned I needed to be beyond myself, to be for family, for friends, for community. **This is where I found my success.**

"You can get everything in life you want if you will just help enough other people get what they want. "

Zig Ziglar

START RISING

How would you define success?

_____

_____

_____

_____

Do you have 3-5 year goals for success? What are they? If you don't, write some ideas down here:

_____

_____

_____

_____

_____

_____

_____

Chapter Ten

Legacy

When I was a young man, I didn't think about what having a legacy meant. Most of us don't when we are in our teens and twenties. We're too busy making a path for ourselves, and learning how to get around in the world. Especially having come to the United States as a teenager, my concerns weren't about what my legacy would be. They were really about surviving and getting to know my new country.

Of course, I knew the word, and what it meant. But I didn't really understand or internalize the concept of legacy until I got a little older, and a lot more mature. It evolved as I evolved, and changed as I changed. I realized that it's important, especially as you bring people into your circle, to leave some sort of footprint or positive mark on the world.

Having children, of course, was an incredible change in my life, and an honor. Holding them when they were tiny babies was amazingly humbling, and those moments help you realize what your real role in life is. It's not to be famous, or rich, or "successful." It's to leave a lasting impression on those you love and care about. It's to make sure that you are being a good person, and contributing positively to your community and family. It's to establish a living legacy of how we can be in this world.

Being an immigrant magnifies this for me. Having come to the United States and being a "foreigner" in this country made me want to be something more. I love this country, as I've said many times, and I wanted to make sure that I didn't just leave a legacy for my family and immediate community. I also want to create a positive legacy for those immigrants who come after me. What can I give to them to help them through the struggles of coming to a new country? A country where they don't know the language, culture, traditions, and expectations of people who live here.

When we consider legacy, we have to think about what we are leaving behind. What part of us will remain with family, friends, community members, and the country we care about after we are gone. Thinking beyond yourself, and looking at what we can give back that will outlast our physical presence. I will admit that this way of looking at things didn't come naturally to me. As I was learning my way in a new country, I was more worried about getting by and succeeding, than leaving a legacy. Fortunately, I stretched my learning by reading books, and surrounding myself with mentors who helped me to see beyond myself, and my immediate needs.

When we think of people who have written seminal books, or left behind generation-defining art, they have lived beyond their years. They have left a gift of themselves, in whatever format they worked in, for us to read, enjoy, and learn from, well past their lifetime. So, the question becomes, what do you want your legacy to be? What will you leave behind, past your time here on earth?

My parents instilled in me a strong sense of survival. My mom, in particular, was great about making sure that we had money put away. This is a trait that I've picked up over the years. But, this sense of survival is not akin to creating and manifesting a legacy. It goes much further than just "getting through," or "surviving." The notion of legacy is often hard to define, and, honestly, I think that some of the best legacies were left by brilliant people who maybe weren't even aware or conscious that they were leaving behind a legacy.

In some ways, a legacy is self-created. It almost comes together as we go through life, and live our lives. As we mature and learn to focus less on ourselves, and more on the needs and dreams of others. The legacy that we leave isn't necessarily something that you write down and set out to do. Sometimes the most powerful legacy that you can leave is the legacy that you lived well, that you treated people well, that people felt important and valued in your presence.

But, sometimes the most important way to achieve that type of success in life is to take note of it, and understand that it can be a goal of yours. That you can shoot for that type of legacy, simply by being aware of it, and understanding that every action you take will either work for, or against any legacy that you may want to leave. We are all 100% responsible for our actions and reactions to the world. So, being aware of what type of legacy we want to leave can go a long way toward creating a lasting and meaningful legacy.

As I became a father, naturally, I did start to think about this. I saw life differently, as most of us do when we have children. We want to help our children make their way through this world, so when we learn something, we want to teach that to our children. Over the years, I would guess that I've written down almost 30 pages of notes to my children -- little life lessons, if you will. I know that when they are young they won't necessarily see or value these notes as a type of legacy that I want to leave for them. But, as they grow older, have families of their own, and experience the ups and downs of life, I think the lessons will mean more to them. They will be establishing their own legacy, as they make their way through their own lives.

My son, for example, is just sixteen as I write this. Every time he and I go over these notes, he picks up a little more and a little more. As he gets older, I can see that more of what I've written makes more sense to him, and becomes more relevant. We all remember our teenage years as sometimes difficult, so, it's my hope that some of what I've written down for him and my other children can be helpful as he sorts things out on his own.

One of the things I've shared with my children is that you can have whatever you want, as long as you do whatever it takes. In some ways, this is the crux of the legacy that I hope to leave for my children. I guess in many ways, also, that's the whole point of this book. To help other immigrants understand that everything is possible in this country -- there is no one holding you down or holding you back. What you get out of your experience and time in this country has everything to do with what you are willing to do and make for yourself.

Do your beliefs and values work toward creating a positive legacy that you can leave your children, your family and your community? Are you defending those beliefs and living what you say are your beliefs? When you are gone from this earth, will people think of you as an upstanding citizen, and one who lived by their word, and was true to those around you? Are you a good example for those around you? When you lay your head down on your pillow at night, and reflect on what you did and who you were that day, are you living up to the legacy that you want to leave?

I tell members of my team to think about this, too. It's not just about who you want to be for your kids and family, but what kind of imprint you want to leave on the lives of your clients and colleagues. When we truly care about the people we work for and with, we can guarantee that we help them feel good at the end of the day, too.

One of my agents was outstanding at this. He would make sure that a client had everything they needed, well past the closing date of the purchase of their new house, for example. He made them feel that he valued not just their business, but their presence in his life -- and, he truly did. He made them feel special, because they were special to him. He knew that he helps people's dreams come true, and that was part of the legacy that he wants to leave.

Winning and losing is a part of life. But, at the end of the day, the most important thing, I think, is to know that I put everything on the table. When we fail, which I have done many times, we need only to look at that as a learning experience. It's only a failure if we don't learn from our losses and misses. Knowing that I did everything I could do, and tried to make my world, my family and my community a better place -- better than I found it -- helps me know that the legacy that I will be leaving will be a positive one. And, I hope, my legacy will be one that my family and kids are proud of.

A legacy isn't always positive, right? Someone's legacy, what they leave behind, can be destructive and negative. This is why it's so critical to reflect on what you do and say every day. Is it contributing to a positive legacy or a negative legacy? Are you honoring your family? Your colleagues? Your clients? Are you defending your positive legacy? Are you consistently proving yourself and your notion of a positive legacy that you want to leave behind for those around you?

Sometimes you know you're going to leave a lasting positive legacy when you are actively being attacked by others. You have raised your hand up, and you are being noticed. It's a sign of success, oftentimes, when people see you as a threat, because they are living a negative life, and leaving a negative legacy. You are competition to them, and you are shining a light on them that they don't like to see in themselves -- they're just not mature enough to understand and admit it.

A few years ago, in 2016, I attended a seminar through The Next Level Experience where we were brought to a cemetery. As we gazed over the graveyard, wandering through, reading the tombstones, we were asked to write our own eulogy. I took a seat in the grass, and wrote, and wrote and wrote. What will be my legacy? I was thinking of what my wife would say about me. What would my kids say about me? Was I living in a way that they would say I was a good husband, a good father, a good member of the community? What would they say I accomplished in my life?

If you're an immigrant to the United States, and you believe in the legacy of this country, that the American Dream is attainable, it's your responsibility to make sure that dream is available to those who come after you. The next generations of immigrants will keep this country going strong. We all add our footprints to the history of this great country. Add yours in a way that will make your family, friends and community proud.

START RISING

Write your eulogy from the point of view of the person you love the most:

_____

_____

_____

_____

_____

_____

_____

_____

_____

_____

_____

_____

_____

Final Thoughts

A Life of Adventure

I've always lived a life of adventure, from studying martial arts, to traveling around the world, from scuba diving to race car driving. Just the other day, I went whitewater rafting, with three broken ribs, after flipping my ATV. I think that sense of adventure has helped me build a stronger mindset and a tough mentality that has helped me get through and thrive in my new country. I don't let things get me down, and I don't worry about too much.

I try not to sweat the little things, and not let those things really stress me out and drain me. That life of adventure, that adrenaline rush that comes from doing exciting things, has helped me understand how to get through tough times, and enjoy the simple pleasures in life as well.

Find something that makes you feel alive. Whether it's sailing a boat in the open ocean, flying an ultralight, or skydiving, what is it that makes you feel alive? What gives you that immense sense of adventure and mastery over everything around you? Experiences more than things bring you this vitality. Purchasing things doesn't cut it. Spend your money on what can help you understand that feeling of adventure. These experiences in life become important as you get older.

Imagine yourself sitting around your grandchildren. They ask you about what you did in life. Do you want to list off things that you bought, or do you want to tell them about your adventures, your mishaps, and your triumphs in life?

Life is short. At any moment, you may be tested in a way that makes you see the real value of life. During a trip to Cancun, not that long ago, I went scuba diving in an amazing reef. The waters were crystal -blue, warm, and luxurious. It was truly an outstanding moment in time.

I was following our tour guide who was swimming in, through, and around the reefs. It was incredibly glorious, and I found myself lost in the moment. It's important to revel in moments like these where we see the beauty all around us, and the complete fragility of life. Scuba diving is inherently a dangerous sport. There is no room for making mistakes. It would only take a split second to get stuck in a space that I could not get out of. There were times during that dive, where things were very tight, all around me, and despite my years of experience, I felt panic coming on as I wondered if I would be able to make it through. Even those times of panic can be life-threatening for a scuba diver.

It's not that I cheated death during that dive, but it was certainly a defining moment for me. I had to trust our guide to take me places that I wouldn't have gone on my own. I had to trust my abilities, and my level-headedness to get me through potentially dangerous situations. I had to have faith that this moment in life was going to be a wonderful memory someday, while I was living through the nerve-testing immediacy of it.

There's no turning back in life. Once you commit to a skydive, for example, you can't change your mind mid-fall and head back up into the plane. You can't just swim up quickly when you're scuba diving, or you can make yourself very sick. When I've flown ultralight aircraft, once you are in the air, or committing to getting in the air, you can't just stop and say, "Oh, never mind."

Life is about going full force through any obstacle that you might run into or any complication you might have. Once you commit to your life, and to what it takes to reach your goals, your best strategy is to keep looking forward and take things head on. "Maybe" doesn't get you very far in life. Adventures require saying "yes," more often than you say, "no."

When you skydive, there's a moment where you're sitting at the doorway of the plane, poised to jump. Sometimes that moment feels like a split second, sometimes it feels like it takes hours. But, at the end of that moment, you have to decide. Do you go, or do you not? Do you jump, or do you live in fear? Do you create a life of adventure, or a life of boring safety? Do you want to keep moving, or be stuck?

This isn't meant to say that you should just jump blindly. No, every time I have put myself out there, either on a sporting adventure, or just making a difficult decision that might put my finances or career at risk, it was with training, expertise, and support. I didn't go skydiving for the first time by thinking I could just slap on a parachute and jump out of a plane. I didn't go diving in that amazing reef in Mexico without a guide and good supports above the water.

A life of adventure doesn't mean you go it alone. *Having mentors, coaches, and teachers to help you on your way, is vital.* My life of adventure was, to a great degree, possible because of wise people who came before me, or who lived the adventure before me. We are not born naturally capable to do much of what life demands. So, having these guides help us out, and give us a hand up when we need, is the key to our success. Most of the time, if we're being honest with ourselves, we couldn't go it alone. My experience has been that most people want to see you succeed, and those who have traveled the path prior to you showing up are usually open to sharing with you what to do, and what to avoid.

I highly recommend that you tap into **coaches** that can help you. This can be someone who is working in your field, or it can be through books, workshops, and seminars. Every time you explore and question what success can mean for you; you will get something out of it that you couldn't have done yourself.

There are so many people that I admire, and who have helped me on my life of adventure. Some are personal friends and close family members. Others are known in the world of entrepreneurship and leadership. Sometimes it only takes somebody saying something to you to really put things in perspective, and open your eyes to what your possibilities and potential are.

Dennis Waitley, author of Seeds of Greatness, once said, "Don't dwell on what went wrong. Instead, focus on what to do next. Spend your energies on moving forward, toward finding the answer." We can all understand that. How sometimes life makes us feel that we are stuck, or we get scared to move forward. But a life of adventure demands that we gather our energies, and move forward. Always.

Jack Campfield, in my opinion is one of the best motivational writers ever and has a quote that has inspired me throughout the years. Because a life of adventure is not just about physical adventures, but also intellectual and emotional adventures. It can be about who you spend time with, and what they show you. It can be about learning new things, and exposing yourself to new knowledge. During one of Jack's live events, I was introduced to a quote from Charlie "Tremendous" Jones. According to Charlie, "You will be the same person in five years as you are today except for the people you meet and the books you read."

You probably know of Jack from his books, starting with *Chicken Soup for the Soul* as his best-known title. Not exactly screaming of adventure as I've described it, however Jack speaks to a deeper adventure that we all need to explore: the adventure of knowing yourself and being yourself. He encourages the knowledge of knowing how to maximize your potential on all levels; professional, personal, spiritual, and physical. A life of adventure can often be found and nurtured in reading work like Jack's.

Living a life of adventure is about living your passions. On the surface, for example, it may not appear that a life career in real estate is living my passion, but it is. I get to help people, and I get to live my own life of adventure. When you try to find a jumping point for your life of adventure, maybe you can get started by asking yourself one simple question...

"What do you care most about?"

As this book has come together, and I've considered what to include, it all comes down to this theme of a life of adventure. Being an immigrant is, in and of itself an adventure, but that's not what has brought me the success

I've experienced in life, so far. What's brought me my success is that spirit of adventure, and living a life of adventure.

How can you do this? What steps should you take? And, though it might seem a little unusual to outline the steps to live your life of adventure, every magnificent journey starts with a few simple steps, right? Enjoy the challenges and embrace them. It is my pleasure to provide some ways to start living your very own life of adventure, in your new way of life. In a very real way, these steps sum up the message of my book, and I hope these steps help you **Rise in America**!

Step 1: Look for the Best in Everyone You Meet

My experience, overall and overwhelmingly, has been to give everyone you meet the benefit of the doubt. For me this includes teachers I had in school when we first moved here, mentors who helped me learn the business, or instructors and coaches who sometimes, literally, taught me how to swim. In general, you can trust people, and trust the intuition you feel about someone when you meet them. Even if that trust is broken, you've learned a valuable lesson and life. As I've mentioned previously, life is short. Treat people like you want to be treated, and often, they will give back tenfold.

Step 2: Explore new places -- travel!

I think it's sad when I meet someone who has never really left where they were born and grew up. Of course, sometimes it's hard to do if you don't have the monetary resources, but I think that can also be just an excuse, sometimes based in fear. Exploring different countries and cultures will help you learn about things like different languages, foods, traditions, and even a feel for a culture. Traveling sheds a different light on your own life. You might go to a different part of the country and see things in a completely different way. For example, in many Latin American countries, you kiss each other lightly on the cheek when meeting. It's a very warm culture, where the United States can be a little more formal. But, this is what life is about. It's about seeing new things, and experiencing new things. Adventure begins when you step out of your comfort zone, and sometimes that means literally traveling to a different part of the world.

Step 3: Be Authentic

The more real, genuine, and true you can be, the easier you will find it to live a life of adventure. You'll be able to soar when you live a life without lies, bad intentions for others, and free from jealousy. Being honest with yourself and with others is easy. Telling lies, and keeping those lies takes more energy than its worth, and it takes away energy that you will need to soar and fly in your life. Building a reputation around being honest will leave a lasting legacy that your family will be proud of. This legacy of honesty will also bring you financial success, as business partners and clients will be drawn to you, because they know that they can trust you. Your life of adventure comes from being honest and real.

Step 4: Be Spontaneous and Creative

It goes without saying that you can hardly live an adventurous life without being spontaneous and creative -- they go hand in hand, and you can't have one without the other. Stop planning all the time! Sure, it's great to plan things out, like taking that big trip to Europe, for example. But, don't plan every minute of every day; that's not an adventure -- that's just a tour. Be willing to book a last-minute trip, or accept the dinner invite from the stranger you just met when asking for directions. I have a friend who went on an epic backpacking trip in the highlands of central Mexico, just because they asked a Facebook friend what they recommended doing while they were in the country. Don't be afraid to do something last-minute that will make you feel alive and free.

Step 5: Love Your Life

Chances are, you're already living an adventure. Think back on risks you've taken to get to where you are in life. You've made your way through ups and down, and have made your life better. Don't compare your adventures to my adventures, or to the Joneses Make your adventures your own, and learn to love your life. That doesn't mean there isn't room to make changes in your life, but just remember that you don't have to change everything in your life to see the adventures you're already living. Cherish what you have, and smile through good times and bad. Adventures are very rarely comfortable all the time. Most of the time, the greatest adventures we have had have come at some kind of cost. But, they make us who we are, and loving our life for what it is right now, in addition to what it can become, is the key to embracing adventure in your life.

Step 6: Surround Yourself with Adventurers

You already know that some people empower you, and support you, and others don't. There are many other people out in the world who will support you taking risks, and living an adventurous life. They have things that they can show you, and you can show them a thing or two, as well. What I've found in my life is that when I'm around adventurous people, my energy increases, and so does theirs. Being around people who inspire you and who make you want to be a bigger, better person, can be the difference to shrinking as you go through life, or expanding your energy. Be that for others, too. Celebrate when they succeed in their adventures, and be happy for them. Support others who are living their dream, just as they support you living yours.

Step 7: Let Go

What does letting go have to do with being adventurous? Well, sometimes this is literal, right? It can mean letting go of the side of the boat to jump into the water and go snorkeling or scuba diving. Letting go of the ledge to leap to another place where you can continue to climb up that mountainside. Letting go of the door of the plane, so that you can freefall downward to the earth.

But, sometimes letting go is more figurative. Letting go of fears that have been holding you back in life. Letting go of the insecurity of being in a new country and not knowing the language. Letting go of people who hurt you, and who don't believe in you.

When you let go, you free yourself to move forward. You free yourself from the ground that has been holding you down, and you truly can soar upward. Letting go doesn't have to feel like a downer or a negative thing. If you think of it where you are just leaving a situation that is holding you back, so that you can move into a better situation, it can become easier.

Sometimes you have to let go of money. Years ago, I was looking at a sleek, expensive sports car. It was too much, I thought to myself. But, a friend leaned over and said, "You know, whatever you don't spend, your children will." I laughed, but got his point. Live your life as you want to now and let go of the voices that are telling you, "It's too much."

Living a life of adventure is what Rising in America is all about. We all have our own path, and our own adventures to take. With the right support, the right education and training, the right preparation, and some safety equipment, we can do just about anything.

I hope that this book has been a support for you. I can't tell you how much my life in America has meant to me. I am forever grateful to my parents for being willing to bring me here, so that I could have the opportunities that I never would have had in Brazil. I am forever grateful to my own family, friends and colleagues, for helping me Rise in America.

.

Biography

Alex Rezende is a self-made accomplished businessman, an immigrant, and **inspiring Best-Selling Author**.

Alex moved to the United States from Brazil at the age of 18, without speaking any English. He graduated high school and went to work; first in the hospitality industry before building his own successful real estate business.

Alex is married and a father of four, and adrenaline is in his veins. He is a 1st dan Black Belt Tae Kwon Do master, skydiver, scuba diver, race car driver, and instructor. A natural giver, Alex loves to help his family, friends, and the community whenever possible.

Today, Alex wants to share his insights and experiences as an immigrant, to inspire and encourage other immigrants to dream and accomplish their goals.

Acknowledgments

WOW, how else can I start, but by saying how excited I am. I have had so much support and encouragement about writing this book that I am still in awe.

I would like to thank so many people, so I apologize in advance if I forget anyone. I can say that without a doubt every one of you have had a great impact in my life.

From my wonderful and caring mother Virginia Derbridge, and my stepfather Ken Derbridge. My hard-working father Marcos Rezende, and my stepmother Dayane Rezende who took me in her house at a difficult age. My sisters Giovana, Janaina, Marjorie, and Bruna. My amazing beautiful girls Kendall, Kaitlyn, Layla, and my joyful and funny son Xander who inspire me every day. My niece Tainah, my nephews Breno and Thiago. To Elmer Justice, Danny Barry and Kathy Bentley for their continuous support.

My team, my business partner Mario Negron, Monica Jimenez, Hanan Jamous, Elier Figueroa, Valerie Cruz, Brandi Adam, Sandra Taylor, Stephen Myshrall, Lisa Vo, and Joao Correa.

All of our other agents at Re/Max Pioneers, current and past ones as they have all contributed towards our growth.

My book manager, Mike Fallat, who has been incredible to work with and Tony Whatley, bestselling author and friend, who introduced me to Mike.

My friends and mentors, this one is where I know I will be missing people for sure, if you felt like if forgot you, maybe we haven't connected in a while and need to ☺.

My brothers from another mother, Alex Sung, John Gunter, Jason Wolf, Cris Sherman, Kin Li, Will Sheen, James Wilkerson, Juan Kirby, Adrian Alonzo, German Vazquez, Brad Whitfill, Cidão, Ossada, Marcelo Itak, and Joe Schirmer.

My extended family of aunts and uncles, my Grandma Dora she is more than a grandma, she is the one I could always go to for anything. My Tio Neto who has been there for me in most of the hardest times of my life. My Tia Cecilia, Tio Leo, Tia Walkiria, my caring Tia Ana my cousins Bernardo, Carolina, Renata, and Mylena.

All my car family, Lamborghini Owner Club, Ferrari Club of America and Porsche Club of American friends and instructors who volunteer a lot of their time to share their wealth of knowledge and experience, especially Steve Bukoski, Tra Townsend, Jeff Lent and others.

To my all my Ginger Racing Teammates, especially our Captain Vann Duke.

To my entire Marriott Family, Jo-Anne Swensson, David Khey, Jennifer Webster, Lisa Whatley, Sheron Jones and many others.

To ALL my clients who have trusted us with one of their most expensive and stressful life events -- buying or selling their homes. I am forever thankful and grateful for being part of it.

To my Tae Kwon Do sensei Master Song, you sir are a great example, and a very positive influence on so many people every day.

To my builder partners, New Home Salespeople and management, plus our vendors and contractors.

Most importantly to my wife "Queen MFB" Linda Rezende, your love, support, drive, and so many other qualities have allowed us to live the life beyond anyone's dreams. I love you my G!

Photo Gallery

Blessed

Ginger Racing Team – Spawn of Chucky

Dreams Do Come True!
at Circuit of The America during PCA event.

My family.

Made in the
USA
Columbia, SC